She Bathed in Moonlight

and

Waltzed with Sins

Ollie Vera

ISBN – 9798368246161

Editing by: Your Writing Table (www.yourwritingtable.com)
Artwork/Illustrations by: Fatima S.

Contact info:
Instagram - @ollieveralyrics
Facebook – Ollie Vera Lyrics and Poetry

Dedication

This is dedicated, with love,

to my amazing Mom, Roseann.

Mom, you always supported my writing,

and I will forever be grateful for

the time we had together.

I miss you everyday and I hope

I am making you proud.

I love you.

TABLE OF CONTENTS

Watch Over Me 11

She Bathed in Moonlight and Waltzed with Sins 12

You Will Still Find Me Fighting 13

Puzzles For Eyes 14

I Didn't Forget 15

And Now I'm Deformed 16

Extinct Laughter 17

Decorate My Wounds with Bones 18

You Matter My Darling 19

I'm Trapped 20

I've Been Walking for A Long Time 21

My Bad Wolf Gets Hungry Too 22

Her Halo Turned to Dust 23

Just The Way It Goes 24

Angels In Black Gowns 26

I Yelled to The High Heavens 28

She Screamed and The Earth Tore Open 30

Except A Cigarette 32

A Loss That'll Make Me Crazy 33

The Lonely Road 34

While She Walks in White 36

As She Enters the Wild 38

But I Never Showed Up 39

I'm Not Afraid of Dying 40

The Trigger 41

Before the Sky Went Gray 42

Only the Good Die Young 43

I Am the Hurricane 44

A Single Red Rose 45

After It All 46

Love Will Make Liars of Us All 48

Take A Bath in Gasoline 49

Everything I Lack 50

Wait for Help to Come 51

Watching the Rain 52

Mama, Can I Lay in Your Arms 53

Night Noises 54

Good Morning to the Afternoon 55

I Am the Water 56

Suddenly Starved 58

Just to See You 59

I Miss You 60

Calling My Name 63

Sit and Watch the Lake 64

You Had to Change on Your Own 65

The Night is a Friend that I Have Earned 66

About the Poet 67

Watch Over Me

My mother

Sweet mother

Beautiful mother

I love you, my mom.

You are the sky

That I look to when I'm lost

You are the light

That the sun cannot live without.

You are the Earth

I played on as a child

And you are the scent

That the rose holds close.

You are the music

That rain makes on tin

And you are my mother

And forever will be.

Rest easy now my mother

And watch over me.

She Bathed in Moonlight
and Waltzed with Sins

She bathed in moonlight

And waltzed with sins.

Every flower petal vibrant with adoration for her.

She drank from poisons

And dealt in fate

Tempting the darkness

With laughter betrayed.

She was beauty and chaos

And mud-covered hope

She was haunted and humbled

An ethereal soul.

Cursed to search the forevers

Longing

Unrested

Untethered

Alone.

You Will Still Find Me Fighting

I didn't need saving

I just forgot

I wasn't breaking

Just a little lost.

I'm here because of the times my heart sank

And I kept going.

I have yet to reach a battle I cannot fight.

Although I may get tired

And my jaded jaw may lose its bite

Up, I will be rising.

You will still find me fighting.

Puzzles For Eyes

Is it the weight of my secrets that has rotted my soul?

The terrible burden of whispers untold

A dreadful concoction of silence and night.

A wandering child with puzzles for eyes.

Is it from hiding in darkness that extinguished my flames?

The veil of this knowledge has rotted my brain.

Combining a secret with an endless fight

A wandering child with puzzles for eyes.

I Didn't Forget

She had black hair
And a blue dress
She walked like thunder
And her life was a mess.

I said goodbye
To a close friend
I walked away
But I didn't forget.

He had a new truck
And a soft voice
A gentle kind of calmness
I didn't know that I liked.

I was drawn to him
And we made mistakes
He broke my heart
And I took the blame.

And Now I'm Deformed

I went in as a child

And came out manufactured

Molded

And folded

And forced to conform.

They said it was the only way how

To escape from the exile

Sculpted

And framed out

And now I'm deformed.

Extinct Laughter

Graffiti on an old barn
Chimneys and those scars
Aging while I fall apart
Hoping while I stand guard.
Extinct laughter
Playing in my mind
Because I remember
All of the good times.
Waiting on a new heart
Maybe just a jumpstart
Watching us like a fast car
Leaving like a shooting star.
Extinct laughter
Playing in my mind
Because I remember
All of the good times.

Decorate My Wounds with Bones

Decorate my wounds with bones

A graveyard of empty coffins

Nobody visits anymore

Left alone and forgotten.

I wake up

Running away from them

Every day I'm

Running from skeletons.

You Matter My Darling

You matter

My darling

Put down the shame

Let it rest.

You matter

My darling

Put down the blame

Let it rest.

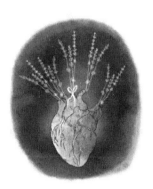

This journey is hard

Made heavier by the pressure.

Stay true in your heart

Stay true through the loss

Keep your candle burning

Reminders of a hope once flickered.

I'm Trapped

If the bite didn't kill me

Then the venom will.

If the wire couldn't hold me

Then this cage sure will.

I'm trapped

Trapped between loving and moving on

I'm trapped

Trapped between a fire and a loaded gun

I'm trapped.

If the walls couldn't hide me

Then the locks just might

If the hope didn't save me

Then the promise might.

I'm trapped

Trapped between the earth and a stormy sky

I'm trapped

Trapped between the truth and a god damn lie

I'm trapped.

I've Been Walking for A Long Time

Loose bricks

Going to make me trip

But I've been walking for a long time.

Broken windows

Going to cut my skin

But I've been walking for a long time.

Cracked cement

Trying to crack my head

I've already said

I've been walking for a long time.

My Bad Wolf Gets Hungry Too

My bad wolf gets hungry too

I chopped up your soul

And I fed it like food

Guilt took me to sleep that night

Guilt took me to sleep last night.

Although, I should feel bad

I feel satisfied.

My bad wolf gets hungry too.

If you want me to act like a princess

Then don't treat me like an animal.

If you want me to bow to every test

Then don't shame me like a sheep for their wool.

Her Halo Turned to Dust

You turned her from an angel to a sinner

The day that you pinned her down.

Her eyes went from gold to black

And you were sitting in the back

The day that you knocked her down.

She'll spend all of her days

Just trying to find her way back now.

Her halo turned to dust

And her white wings to rust

And the screaming's gotten too damn loud.

Just The Way It Goes

Photographs display someone else's past

A man from a world that didn't last.

And I just wish she'd know

I just had to head home.

Lately I've been thinking about

Things that I used to have

Lately I've been thinking about

Things that I couldn't have.

But that's just the way it goes.

That's just the way it goes.

They tell me that now it is the time

Dreading the grind that is the climb

But I just have to have hope.

Lately I've been thinking about

Things that I never had

Lately I've been thinking about

Things that I shouldn't have.

But that's just the way it goes.

That's just the way it goes.

Counting the seconds that tick on by

Praying to God that they don't ask why.

But I guess I'm kind of screwed.

Awaiting a rain from a cloudless sky

Praying to God that they don't ask why

But I guess I'm kind of screwed.

Angels In Black Gowns

Angels in black gowns
And halos of fire.
Walking down these streets
And losing desire.
Hoping for a love
That will take them higher.
But knowing that all love
Will make you a liar.

I Yelled to the High Heavens

Half of me is asleep
And the other half is buzzing free
Trying to get to where I'm going
But I don't know where that might lead.

I slipped through the cracks
Once before this time
It was as far as I could fall
While still holding my glass of wine.

I yelled to the high heavens
But all I heard back were sighs
I guess they agreed with you
That I'm not really worth their time.

Rock bottom's looking pretty good right now
And if you let me stay
I promise I won't make a sound.

Maybe if I crawl
I can keep from being loud.

But not much is going to keep me

From falling to the ground.

I yelled to the high heavens

But all I heard back were sighs

I guess they agreed with you

That I'm not really worth their time.

Is this bed free for me to finally rest my head?

I'd lay down alone

But it's too crowded in my bed.

Awakened by my demons

Cause they said they haven't yet been fed.

I'd have fed them long ago

But I thought they all were dead.

She Screamed and The Earth Tore Open

She screamed

And the earth tore open

Hell climbed through.

Demons came crawling

When Hell broke loose.

She fell to the ground

And the sky tore open

Hail poured through

The thunder was rumbling

And the lightening too.

One can be broken

And still go on the same

Although she was warned

It seemed that nothing changed.

She cried

And the stars burst open

The dark shone through

The light fell silent

And her tears did too.

One can be broken
And still go on the same
Although she was warned
It seemed that nothing changed.
He broke
And the tide poured through him
And took him away
Although he was scared
it was a safer place.

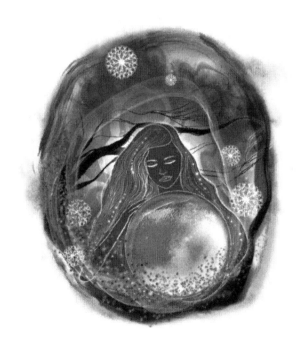

Except A Cigarette

I have everything I want

Except a cigarette.

I fell through twice

And no one knows where I went.

I walk the dungeon halls, every now and then.

Though I know I'll never be locked up again.

A Loss That'll Make Me Crazy

This is a love that leaves me lonely
A loss that'll make me crazy
But I just can't help but hold on.

Alone again, turn on the TV,
Bring the dogs inside and cuddle my cat.
Distractions just aren't working
I can't forget about you just like that.

A burning feeling I can't escape.
A battle that I just can't fight.
A smile that I just can't fake.
And I see no end in sight.

This is a love that leaves me lonely
A loss that'll make me crazy
But I just can't help but hold on.

The Lonely Road

There's only one way to go

That's the lonely road

I fell on stones

I scraped my knees

I broke my bones.

But I kept going down

The lonely road.

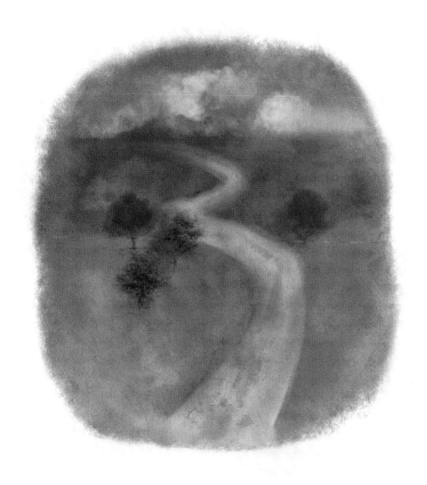

While She Walks in White

She stood on a bridge

Early one morning

Her hair all around her

And the river was flowing.

She wore a white dress

And still a wedding veil

I never could guess

What she was doing there.

Some say she walks the forest

Unseen but not alone

Hand in hand with her loneliness

She tries to find the one.

I heard the story of that day

She had been painted like snow

Her heart was hers to give away

But his heart broke her own.

She followed the church path

Down to the water

To this same bridge

As if it called her.

Nobody knows what happened next

How her spirit came to find

In this forest, her love's final rest.

While she walks in white.

.

As She Enters the Wild

She put flowers in her hair as a child

She picked them away from the earth

And the leaves that fell, she piled

Drawn to nature from birth.

Nature is though, you know

That one day, everything goes

Though it wasn't nature that took her

Too far away from this land.

Now the ocean is her mirror

And the earth is her nightstand.

She can use the stars as her glitter

That she put in her hair as a child

And the horizon is her beacon

As she enters the wild.

But I Never Showed Up

Took off down the road

Said I was heading home

But I never showed up.

They lied on the map

Said I'd find my way back

But I never showed up.

They waited for me

I heard they waited days

But I never showed up.

Disappointment on her face

While she silently prayed

That I wouldn't show up.

You see, I've been travelling

Trying to find my sense of home

But things have held me back

Pinned me down so I couldn't keep going.

You see, I've walked

And I've walked

And I've started

And I've stopped.

Too bright in the day

I walk at night

Trying to make it home

Down this damn road.

.

I'm Not Afraid of Dying

I'm not afraid of falling down
I'm afraid of coming back around
And the path in which I used to lie
Has begun to fade with dying time.
I used to welcome the sunshine
Now I am blinded by the flames
I used to be so sure of my mind
Now I have thoughts I cannot tame.
And with every breath I take
I get closer to the end
But I'm not afraid of dying
More of coming back again.

The Trigger

I heard the trigger
But I didn't hear the shot
I heard the trigger
But I didn't step in front.
I heard the thump
Of the body to the ground
But I didn't hear the bang
That brought the body down.

Before The Sky Went Grey

Just tell me what the sunshine looked like

Before the sky went grey

Tell me of the taste of the rays

Tell me of the warmth against your back

And the hope it put into your day.

Cause the sky won't stop raining now

And the atmosphere is of black clouds.

I'm trying to find my faith

But I just keep finding rain.

Only The Good Die Young

It was when my knees hit the floorboards

My palms hit the wood

That everything I ignored

I finally understood.

Only the good

Die young.

It was with tears in my eyes

Stains on my shirt

That everything I ignored

I finally understood.

Only the good

Die young.

I Am the Hurricane

You are the venomous snake

And I am the earth you camouflage into.

You are the disaster

And I am the ocean that won't flood.

You are the mountain lion

And I am the fire that scares you away.

You are the wind sighing

And I am the hurricane.

A Single Red Rose

A single red rose

Beside her while she sleeps

A letter on the nightstand

In case she never wakes.

A single dry tear

Lies still on her cheek

Hope in her mind

That it will be okay.

Fear has taken her mind
again

And it holds her tight

Tears have taken her eyes
again

And they kiss her goodnight.

It is dark outside

And cold out the window

She quiets her mind

With a rose on her pillow.

After It All

Can you do me a favour

After it all

Don't turn around

Until after I'm gone.

Can you close your eyes

For just a minute

And I'll pretend

I'm a secret.

I'll slip away

From your lips

Quietly

Without a kiss.

Goodbyes can be difficult

So let's not try

Just close your eyes dear

I'll get the lights.

My heart so heavy

I plan the escape

Slowing my breathing

I slip away.

You'll open your eyes

And I'll be gone

But thanks for the favour

After it all.

.

Love Will Make Liars of Us All

He was always there

When she needed him

He'd stroke her hair

And pull her closely in.

Time went on

And she fell hard

So in love

And not scared at all.

But then I watched him tell her

She didn't matter

And I watched her walk away

Later she told me

It didn't matter

She never cared about him anyway.

Love will make

Liars of us all.

Love will make

Liars of us all.

Take A Bath in Gasoline

Take a bath in gasoline
And dance next to a fire
Make a bracelet with no beads
And a necklace made of wire.
Give me a day filled with night
And a night filled with sun
A lantern with no light
And a life of only one.
Free my doves to the ground
To fly with the roots
Let go of right now
And the future too.
Hold my anger in your palms
And fix my broken soul
Don't catch me if I fall
I can't do this anymore.

Everything I Lack

Make me a painting
Of pale blue colours
Cause I hate reflecting
I avoid all mirrors.
Draw me a shadow
But don't shade it black
And don't make it follow
Everything I lack.
Create me some eyes
That have never seen tears
Of a painful goodbye
Throughout their years.

Wait For Help to Come

Working towards it all falling down

Bringing myself towards crashing

Swimming to bring me to drown

I find my grip but never latching.

I reach a crevice in the cliff

That I've been falling from

I grab a hold of its lip

And wait for help to come.

Watching The Rain

You always thought it was strange

How much I loved watching the rain

You hated it so much

You'd always complain

It messed with your hair

It messed with your day.

Now think of me when the rain falls down

Notice the magic when it leaves the clouds

Listen for my words in the pouring sound

And feel my love when it soaks the ground.

Mama, Can I Lay in Your Arms

Mama, can I lay in your arms

Like when I was a child

And can you wrap your arms around me?

I'm all alone

And I'm out in the world

And I'm trying so hard to be happy.

Mama, can you sing me a song

A sweet lullaby

Like you did when I was young?

I'm hoping and praying

It's all going to be okay

But things have gotten really tough lately.

And you're not here to protect me.

Night Noises

Night noises are constant

My window is open for them to come through

The coyotes howl in the distance

And in the tree, the owl hoots.

My curtain dances with the wind

Creating shadowed patterns on the wall.

My strength is running thin

But I know I cannot fall

Right outside, I know the sun will rise

And the morning birds will sing their songs

Though I almost fear the morning light

Cause I can't hear the noises of the dark.

I have no shape

No colour

I am merely a reflection

Of the trees

Of the skies

Of the storms

Of the faces. All the faces.

You can contain me, yes

But I'll escape

Turn to condensation

Or evaporate

You can't hold me too tight

I'll slip away.

You can only listen

To the noise I make

When I fall as rain.

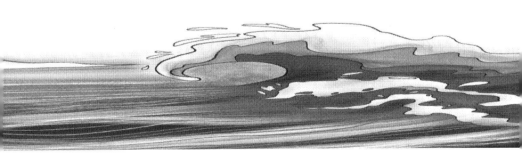

Suddenly Starved

I always believed in love

Until you showed me hate

I always believed in good

Until you showed me evil.

Now there is a violence

That I can't escape

It is vicious

It is brutal

It's a fed lion

That is suddenly starved.

Just To See You

If I could swim to the bottom of an ocean

Just to see you

You know I would swim to the bottom.

I'd look up to see the sun shining through the water

If I could see the sun at all.

Right now, I look up, and the sun is easy to spot

The skies are so blue

I love it

But I don't see you.

Maybe if I swim to the bottom of an ocean

I would see you

When I look up to see the sun shining through the water

If I could see the sun at all.

I Miss You

I swear I've never been this confused

And all I really can do

Is sit on my bed

And stare out my window.

You're a million miles away

I know

But I miss you.

I look at the moon

It's looking back at me

And I think of you.

The stars, they light my way

Like you used to

And I miss you.

The world has brought me down again

I don't know what to do

I'm coming unglued

And I miss you.

Calling My Name

I can hear a noise through the rain

Between the first drop

And the second

There is something calling my name.

Who is calling my name

Through the rain

And rain clouds

Towards the sun?

Between the first drop

And the second

There is something calling my name

Calling me home through the rain.

Sit and Watch the Lake

Sitting here awake

Staring at the lake

Because I cannot sleep

As a willow, I weep.

Wondering what to do next

Wondering what my next move is

If I should say how I feel

How do I know if it's real?

I'll watch the moon dance with the water

Watch the shore drink the waves

I'm not shattered

I'm just dazed

So, I'll sit here awake

Sit and watch the lake.

You Had to Change on Your Own

They tried to tell you that they love you
But you kept saying that they really don't
They didn't want to leave you all alone
But you had to change on your own.
They shouldn't have had to put up with you
When no matter what, you wouldn't move
There was nothing that they could do
When you made sure they would always lose.
You kept thinking it was all a lie
Kept claiming that your heart was shy
You could've listened to their helpful cries
You could've listened before goodbye.
And see how now that it's too late
All you can do is sit and wait
There's nothing that you can fake
When you've already made the sad mistake.
You must've known you'd meet this wall
And wish it didn't happen at all
Now who's going to be there when you crash and fall?
And who's going to respond to your desperate call?

The Night Is a Friend That I Have Earned

It was a long road that I had to walk

But the darkness became my friend along the way

The night told me to trust

And that it's okay to talk

But I stayed silent in the shadows,

I didn't know what to say.

I cried with the night all around me

The stars guided me and told me where to turn.

I didn't know where to go

But now I see

And the night is a friend that I have earned.

Presenting the Poet...

First Nations singer-songwriter, Ollie Vera, uses a blend of strength and vulnerability in her writing that has been captivating readers and listeners alike.

It took quite a bit of courage to create her Instagram page, @OllieVeraLyrics, but when she did, she was amazed how easy it was to share her work. We hear her now wishing she had the courage to share earlier on.

Mental health and life challenges presented themselves and made it difficult for her bravery to shine through. Her daring attitude won in the end, though, grabbing the attention of many artists wishing to help her along her journey.

She now also has a Facebook page, *Ollie Vera Lyrics and Poetry*, dedicated to writing and sharing her art. This is the page that brought Ollie Vera and her editor, Chelsia/Your Writing Table, together!

Ollie Vera grew up on bonfires and horseback riding and is often described as bubbly and shy. At the age of 13, Ollie's lyrics and poetry, touched the hearts of everyone who read them. By 20, she had a music room set up with instruments to really let loose and mess around. Now, at 28, she is expected to continue writing, recording, and growing as a singer songwriter.

You can find Ollie Vera's music on YouTube, Apple Music, Spotify, Amazon Music, Tidal, and TikTok.

Manufactured by Amazon.ca
Bolton, ON

31916360R00037